DIVORCE
in the
CHURCH

MABLE ALYSE MANNING

Copyright © 2017 by MABLE ALYSE MANNING
Los Angeles, California
All rights reserved
Printed and Bound in the United States of America

Published And Distributed By
Mable Alyse Publishing
Los Angeles, California
Email: manningalyse@gmail.com
Website: www.mablealyse.com

Packaging/Consulting
Professional Publishing House
1425 W. Manchester Ave. Ste. B
Los Angeles, California 90047
323-750-3592
Email: professionalpublishinghouse@yahoo.com
www.Professionalpublishinghouse.com

Cover design: TWA Solutions
First printing June 2017
978-0-692-87746-3
10987654321

No part of this book may be reproduced, stored in a retrieval system or transmitted in any form or by any means without the prior written permission of the publisher—except by a reviewer who may quote brief passages in a review to be printed in a newspaper, magazine or journal.

Dedication

I dedicate this book to my daughter, Ryan. May you learn the truth from the truth. May you grow to understand the positive and negative aspects of love and marriage. May you one day meet and unite with the King that God has for you. I pray that you find true love and live happily ever after. May you be a Queen forever. May you multiply and be fruitful, bearing your own beautiful children. My prayer for you is that God will always resonate with you. May your covenant blessings God has for you spring forth in your life.

I also dedicate this book to any person who entered a marriage with the intention of being married happily forever. May God lift you and restore you. I pray a special prayer for anyone betrayed by a spouse. This is another statistic fallen in the hands of the unfortunate epidemic "Divorce."

This book is especially dedicated to "Significant Women" all over the world. May you soon rise above the pain and pitfalls of divorce and depression. This book is for both women and men who have learned and gained knowledge from this tragic experience. I hope that many of you will someday be able to share your stories. I salute you for being a tough trooper. God loves you, and, yes! You are "Significant."

TABLE OF CONTENTS

Acknowledgments 7

Preface 11

Chapter 1: Why do Christians Stay in a Broken Marriage? 15

Chapter 2: The Perfect Picture 25

Chapter 3: Wanting More Than Mama and Daddy Had 29

Chapter 4: High Profile Divorces in the Church 35

Chapter 5: Infidelity 41

Chapter 6: Did You Hear From God? 49

Chapter 7: The Controversy of Marriage and Divorce 57

Chapter 8: The Shame of Divorce in the Church 69

Chapter 9: Embrace Your Singleness 73

Chapter 10: Pieces of Me 81

Chapter 11: Why I Will Never Marry Again 89

Chapter 12: Healing and Feeling Better 95

Conclusion 99

Acknowledgments

First, I would like to thank God for taking me through in 1998, which was undoubtedly the hardest year of my entire life. Thank you, God, for watching over me when I thought I was going to die. Thank you for watching over the fetus I carried while undergoing so much stress. Thank you for allowing her to be born healthy and happy. Thank you, God, again for peace of mind and for keeping a continual praise in my heart and a smile on my face. Thank you, God, for You are the true love of my Life.

Thank you to my mother, Mable, for your constant prayers and guidance. Thank you for never letting go. Even through your cancer diagnosis and dealing with your own issues, you never stopped praying for me. Thank you, Mommy, for always being right there. Thank you for being there when I wanted to take my and my child's life. You prayed me through. I say thank you for giving up your sleepless nights so that my nights would not be sleepless. Thank you for your wisdom, true love, and concern. I thank you, Mommy, for always being a true and perfect example of what all mothers should be. I will always strive to be the kind of mother to Ryan and Andrew that you have always been to me.

To my dad, who has since gone to Heaven, I say thank you for waking up at 4:30 each and every morning to make sure I was safe and off to work.

Thank you to my sisters: Betty, Belinda, and Yvette. You were and have always been around for me. Belinda, you were a great Lamaze partner. Thank you.

Thank you to my nieces and nephews for all your prayers, love, and concern.

Thank you to all my "Girls," who, back then, were right there for the birth of Ryan. I love you all: Toy, Tina, Traci, Debra, Michelle, and Ros. "Thanks for being my friends."

To my god brother, Jerome; thanks for being my "moving man."

Thank you to Sis Althea Sims for being the one person who saw the hurt well beyond my smile. You opened the door to my healing process. You were more than just a First Lady. You were my therapist, and my mentor, who prayed for me constantly. Today, your ministry is yet what many people need. May God continue to use you for His glory.

Pastor Lollis, thank you for always reminding me to bind the devil and to leap for joy.

JB, thank you for all your prayers, love, and support. You have truly been an angel.

I also want to acknowledge inspirational visionaries Joyce Myers, T.D. Jakes, Joyce Rodgers, Dr. Rosie Milligan, Steve Harvey, and the late Myles Munroe. You have inspired me to pursue my purpose and destiny.

Preface

To God be the Glory for the Things That He Has Done

At the time of my divorce in 1998, I was no specialist in the arena of marriage and divorce.

I'll admit that it actually took me about fifteen years to write and complete this book.

However, eight years after my divorce, I decided to attend graduate school, earning a Master's of Science Degree in

Marriage Family Therapy. As a Marriage Family Therapist, I help others to make it through the trials and tribulations of their lives.

Today, I am at a great place in my life. I am the person I am because of God's grace and mercy. Without all the hurt, the tears, and the pain, I would not have become all that I am now. I have come to realize that He was in control the entire time. Not knowing that God had a plan for my life well before I was born, I doubted Him. He was designing and preparing me for what He had intended for me to become all along.

God knew I would become a vessel for Him, helping others to restore their lives, which is what I love to do. God created me to be compassionate to others..

Thank you, God, for being real in my life. I thank You, God, for choosing me to be Your vessel. What the devil meant for evil, God, You meant it for my good. Lord, I thank You for giving me resiliency, determination, and a will to live. Like the saying goes, "What doesn't kill you, makes you stronger."

Lord, help me help others to find their way out of whatever problems they may face.

I wrote this book with empathy to women all over the world, as well as address women who have been hurt and tormented by the traumatic experience, which occurs when couples divorce.

Divorce forces people to transition their entire lives. This is a great read for both men and women, as well as for couples, or individuals, who have plans to marry. You will find that Divorce in the Church is also a great read for individuals who are facing divorce, and for those who might be recovering from divorce. Please use this book as a positive stepping-stone to help you to get your life back on track. For this, too, shall pass.

"Oh, how wonderful life truly is." I am a witness that God can, and will, pull you through it.

Unfortunately, divorce continues to break apart families everywhere. The epidemic of "Divorce" has hit the "Church," with a force as never before. Yes, Christians get divorced, too. And, yes, Christians got issues, too. After all, we are humans, just like everyone else. And, yes, Christians divorce for the same reason that non- Christians divorce. Issues such as cheating (both same and opposite sex), lying, adultery, abuse, inequality, lack of communication, finances, a loss of Identity, intimacy and - affection. For many couples, just the word, "divorce," can be terrifying.

However, divorce continues to strike Christian marriages every day. This heart-wrenching experience can strike at any time, regardless of color, gender, ethnicity, faith, or religion. Divorce strikes mothers, fathers, sisters, brothers, daughters, co-workers, friends, politicians, entertainers…you name it. The trauma of divorce even tends to have a negative impact on the immediate and extended sides of the families.

Chapter 1

Why Christians Stay in a Broken Marriage

I believe Christians often stay in broken marriages because they don't want to disappoint their families, or God. Many simply believe God wants them to stay married. Spouses often say they are committed to God, as well as to their spouses. And, because they are committed, they have faith that God will fix everything and make their marriages all right.

I would like to think most born-again Christians know, and feel, this in their hearts. Christians hope and pray God will heal and restore their marriage, making it even better than before. I would also like to think Christian couples are more willing to seek outside interventions, such as counseling, in hopes of saving and stabilizing the marriage.

The option of throwing in the towel should be the absolute last position that Christians take. After all, marriage is work, and couples should be willing to fight hard to be good at it. Couples must take the time to nurture it. Do not get so caught up with the church that it causes you to start neglecting your marriage.

Back in the day, some of the older Christians and churchgoers lived by some of the "old sayings" or "bylaws" of the church. There is one particular saying that I remember the old folks saying, even when I was a child. It was "Once married always married." This simply meant if a husband and wife divorced and were a part of the church, they could not remarry as long as his/her spouse was still alive. Many former generations also grew up with the notion that "whoever you married, you chose to do so. Therefore, you had made your bed and, despite the consequences, you had to lay in it and stay married forever."

I later learned that this was just an old traditional saying and teaching.

It is funny that divorces were unheard of in the early 1950s. Couples would just deal with whatever, including the not-so-blissful times. Well, being young and not knowing much about marriage, I guess a lot of couples probably stayed together because of this. Misery or not. For love or not.

Another reason why I believe so many Christians stay in broken marriages is because of the kids. They think of the hurt and pain it would cause the children if the family were not a nuclear family anymore. Maybe some couples simply stay together to avoid the embarrassment and shame that goes along with it. There is even more ridicule when a pastor and his wife divorce.

I believe there are probably many pastors who avoided divorce in order to sustain the church's integrity. I would assume when pastors and their wives divorce, parishioners take sides, placing blame on either partner.

Many spouses, I think, put on a "front," or pretend that both their married life, as well as their love for the ministry, is great.

But putting on a show will only last for so long. Unanswered questions will eventually surface, such as:

1. Should Christians stay, even when they know in their hearts that it's over?

2. Should Christian couples talk to others about the failing marriage (such as counselors, other pastors, wives, extended family, etc.)?

3. Should Christian couples separate until they work things out?

4. Should pastors remove themselves from the pulpit until they reckon with their failing marriage?

5. How long should Christians work on their marriage issues before they declare it's over?

6. Should Christians have prenups?

7. Should a pastor, or leader in the church, be required to sit down from leadership positions (during or after the divorce)?

Staying in a broken marriage is not always easy, and neither is leaving. Where there is pressure and stress, decision-making becomes even harder. I do believe, no matter who you are, and what position you might hold in the church, all individuals need to seek counseling, both couple and individual therapy. We are human beings and sometimes we need to talk to someone. Someone to listen, that is, other than God.

I don't think it's hypocrisy if the marriage fails. However, I do think it's wrong when Christian couples don't seize every opportunity to save the marriage. I do believe if you are unhappy, miserable, and have a "true reason" to get out, then do it. Free yourself and run as fast as you can. But, keep this one thought in mind.: there really should never be any Christian divorces, especially when the husband and wife are living according to the word of God. According to Ephesians 5:25 (NIV), "Husbands, love your wives, just as Christ loves the church and gave himself up for her."

Unfortunately, a woman's life seems to change more from divorce than a man's life does. Men just seem to move on with life much faster. Women, being emotional, usually take a bit longer to move on and to heal. Perhaps it's harder for most women to move life forward after a divorce because oftentimes women tend to put off their careers for the sake of the "family."

Some women sacrifice themselves in exchange for a successful family and marriage. Women, being so nurturing, automatically want their husbands to be happy. Women also want their husbands to be happy with them, always. A great marriage is a "high" stake. It's important to win at being a great mother and wife. Although we want it all, we just naturally place ourselves on the "back burner," while losing our own identity.

Our once sought-after careers and lifelong goals seem miles away, almost out of reach, especially when we begin having children. So, when our marriage is in trouble, we start to feel like our options are limited. Women may feel as though "they can't just walk away." After all, they invested too much into the marriage.

This often starts the "whys of life." When things get tough, women often blame themselves. After all, because we kind of let everything else go for the sake of the family. Women find themselves staying in a broken marriage, even when they know the marriage has issues. Many figure it's better than starting life over after such a rewarding, yet time-consuming investment. No one wants an investment to go down the drain.

After speaking with others, couples often view marriage as an investment. Here are a few questions to consider discussing with your spouse or friends.

1. Did I invest enough time into my marriage?
2. Did I neglect to put enough time into my marriage?
3. Has the investment grown?
4. Has the investment fluctuated?
5. Did the investment make any gains?
6. Was this a bad investment?
7. Will I ever get back what I have put in?
8. Have I gotten back more than I have put in?
9. Is the marriage bankrupt?
10. Is it time to cash in my investment, and change markets?

Oftentimes, Christians give the church more energy than they give to their marriages.

Again, I do believe people should live their best life. And before you get married or divorced, pray and seek God. Please, wait to hear from God. Don't make any sudden moves without God's permission. Marriage is one of the most important decisions you will make in life.

Notes

Chapter 2

The Perfect Picture

Have you ever sat in church and wondered where to find your Mr. Right or Ms. Right? Have you ever wished you had a marriage like Brother and Sister Ketchup, or Mr. and Mrs. Mustard has?

Everything looks like it is great. They have a dream-like, movie-type of relationship and marriage. They have the perfect cute little babies. The perfect house, nice cars. In fact, Sister

Mustard doesn't even have to work. She just stays at home and takes care of the kids, goes to yoga, and gets her nails done. This family always goes out to dinner, take nice vacations, wear nice designer clothes, and their kids have big birthday parties every year. You know who they are. They're just always doing something exciting.

All seems to be great with this family. However, don't assume anything because what you see is not always what you see. Well, in fact, even what we think might be a perfect family and marriage is truly not. They've got marital problems, just like anyone else. In other words, the "Perfect Picture" really isn't so perfect after all.

In fact, the picture is about to fall off the wall. It's barely hanging on. It just doesn't look crooked from our angle. The humanistic side of individuals wants the finer things in life. But you should never want, or wish for, what someone might have. And, keep in mind that just because he (it) looks right, acts right, talks right, and dresses right, it doesn't mean he (its) the right one for you.

Sometimes, we want things that are not for us. It's not part of our purpose or plan that God has in store for our lives.

However, God will sometimes allow us to see for ourselves. He will give us what we think we want but don't need. We then have to learn the hard way when we should have waited on God to give it to us. Don't get in God's way. He can do it all by Himself. And, remember, just because Sister Mustard has what you think is the perfect picture life, it might not be at all because it's been raining non-stop in her marriage.

It rains in most cities and countries, regardless of how hot it gets. Think about the tropics. Yes, it rains, and the rain helps to beautify the land. Rain and sun helps plants to grow and makes the land green.

And, like the rain, marital issues help the relationship to grow and develop. A little rain is okay sometimes, for without the rain, the land would be dry and barren and that isn't good either. However, too much rain can lead to many problems, such as floods, mudslides, fungal growth, and erosion, just to name a few ecological imbalances.

Notes

Chapter 3

Wanting More Than Mama and Daddy Had

As the saying goes, everybody wants "more." This also equates to wanting more than what our parents had. It's funny because most parents want their children to have a better life, and actually more than what they had. We all want a better education, a better job, and a better marriage, which all seems to boil down to a better lifestyle.

Back in my parents' generation, couples would hold on to marriages for dear life, regardless of how terrible the marriage possibly was. They held on to that one line in the marriage vows, which said, "Till death us do part."

I will give that generation a hand for that. Now, while the stuff was probably hitting the fan, as the old saying goes, even if "Papa was a rolling stone," and Mama was sleeping with the milk man, they stayed married and always pretended to be happily married in front of the children.

I mean, if there was hatred in the marriage, we, as kids, never saw it. Back then, even though they weren't entirely committed to just each other, they were committed to never divorcing. When I learn of older couples married for like fifty-nine years, I often wonder if they were one of "those" couples I just mentioned. I really wonder how many of those years were great and happy. Was it all just a put on? I wonder if somewhere in their hearts, they actually loved each other. Or were they just sticking it out for the kids.

Well, as time goes on, and "times" change, so have the mindset changes of many of today's married couples. Perhaps because of technology, we view the world now from so many different angles. Persons of my generation have more and better life-changing opportunities. These opportunities often dictate the defining and measuring of one's life by the outlook of others. Higher education and limitless employment opportunities have been the gateway to a better lifestyle. And, with the life of luxury being portrayed everywhere we turn, it makes it hard not to want a better lifestyle than what our parents had.

Magazines, advertisements, television, and especially the depiction of new "reality" shows make the human side crave what they see. Most persons of my generation feel like we want to go to more and better places than our parents did. Some of our parents never had the chance to travel abroad on high-end vacations.

Today, we want finer clothes, jewelry, cars, homes, better bodies, vacations, etc. In today's world, material possessions equate to success. Such items help to persuade and possibly convince others, "We got it going on." Society has placed so much pressure on "having it all together," that some Individuals will do just about anything to obtain "status symbols." And, yes, some will even go as far as marrying a person with whom they share no love, compatibility, etc., but who can provide financial security. Furthermore, some will go to any extreme to have a rich lifestyle. However, sometimes wanting more than "Mama and Daddy had" can put pressure on the marriage.

Wanting more can take a toll on most marriages. Aspiring to greatness and wanting and achieving the best in life is wonderful, but when it burdens the marriage, it quickly causes devastation to the union. Many times, marriages start to suffer when we begin to obtain material items we can't afford and often don't even need. Such behaviors often lead to devastating outcomes, such as bad credit, foreclosures, homelessness, bankruptcy, and so on. These outcomes normally lead straight into divorce.

One might think, Surely, Christians don't measure the success of an individual by what they can see. Well, yes, some actually do measure people's lifestyles by what they see. Most people automatically assume a person or family is doing well by what they see on the outside. Again, the fancy cars, homes, lifestyle.

And, yes, who doesn't want nice things? Now, it's okay to want to have more than our parents might have had. But, just be sure your wanting more is not sacrificing the family or marriage just to fulfill your selfish desires. And, please try not being one of those persons, who always has to show off. Don't always try to keep up with the "Bottle Top family." After all, you really don't know what's really going on with the "Bottle Top family." Remember; what you see might not always be exactly what you see.

I know you are not surprised that the overspending mentality is also very prevalent in the church. Many will stretch their giving in the church while disregarding their bills that are due at home. They use the familiar saying, "God will make a way." While not discerning the fact that the way has already been made.

I can just imagine church folks, saying, "I got more than my mama and my daddy had." And, you better believe many people end up marrying the wrong person for these reasons. Some individuals won't even consider love and compatibility. They just want to be able to live a great life of "luxury."

Don't be a fool and fall in love only with what the marriage can offer you or you will surely end up as a statistic and the epidemic of "divorce" will soon hit you, too.

Notes

Chapter 4

High Profile Divorces in the Church

Today, divorce is a household word. It seems as though everyone is doing it. No one seems to be holding the standards and commitment of marriage. And, yes, even preachers, Sunday school teachers, praise leaders, and worship singers, too.

Yep. Not everyone escapes the divorce epidemic. Many have fallen victim, even a few high profile Christians who are part of popular and mega ministries. I remember many folks talking about those who had fallen victim, just all in a person's business.

I can't even imagine what happens, and how one might feel, when the whole world knows that marriage has failed. Public humiliation, as I could only imagine, is crazy. Okay. So, I see it this way. Have you ever done something that perhaps you were so embarrassed about and hated that a few of your friends or coworkers knew? You probably wondered just how you would face them, and if their perception of you as a person had changed.

Well, just think. This is only a taste of probably how persons of high statures felt when all eyes were on them and their personal lives and divorce. I can only imagine how it feels to have life going great, loving the Lord, and then, Wham, Bam! The Big 'D' strikes with a force, causing more than just the lives of the couples involved to change forever. What about the parishioners? Whose side are you on when it's a pastor and his wife who's calling it quits? What do you think? Should pastors and their wives separate first, in order to work on their issues? Or, should they just pretend and go on as normal, as if there are no real problems? Should they do any of these for the sake of the "Church?"

Divorces tear families apart, and they surely could tear apart a church family. Do parishioners split? Do some go to the left while others go to the right? Well, clearly, some of these ministries lose members all together. Some might draw conclusions based on what they heard, while some might make assumptions of what they believe occurred. Will the ratio of the church numbers change after the divorce? What actually happens?

Well, I will let you answer these questions for yourself. Perhaps you will be able to remember the day you heard that some of the high-profile persons were going through a divorce. For whatever reasons, these individuals chose to end their marriages. Prayers were in full effect that God would help them to sustain and make it through their personal trials of life that became public, right before their eyes.

To name some high-profile church persons who divorced:

1. Juanita Bynum (2008)

2. Yolanda Adams (2004)

3. Hezekiah Walker (2016)

4. Detrick Hadden (2011)

5. Clarence McClendon (2000)

6. Paula White (2007)

7. Jamal Bryant (2009)

8. Dr. Wanda Davis Turner (2005)

9. Benny Hinn (2010)

10. Riva Tims (2009)

11. Jim and Tammy Bakker (1992)

12. Donnie Swaggart (2003)

13. Paul Crouch Jr. (2007)

14. Israel Houghton (2016)

15. Fred Hammond (2004)

16. Derek Webb and Sandra McCracken (2015)

17. Pastor Charles Stanley (2000)

(For more divorces, look up on the Internet.)

Nothing makes these individuals immune from the vicissitudes of life. People forget they are human, too. They have to cry out to God, just like anyone else.

So, whom do we blame for the rise of divorces taking place in churches all across America? "It's nothing but the Devil," as I can hear some old church mother saying inside of my head. Is it the devil? Yes, some might say, while others might think some problems go along with some marriages.

For the scripture says in John 10:10 (NKJV), "The thief does not come except to steal, and kill, and to destroy. I have come that they may have life, and that they may have it more abundantly."

Oh, many times, as saints being humanistic, we fall right into the hands of Satan. As it says in 1 Peter 5:8, "Be sober, be vigilant: because your adversary the devil walks about like a roaring lion, seeking whom he may devour."

Notes

Chapter 5

Infidelity

Infidelity? The question is, "Does it really exist in churches?" The answer is yes. Some Christians are guilty of Infidelity. They break the promise to remain faithful to their spouses along with the vow made to God. Infidelity can be described in several ways, whether it's having a romantic, emotional or sexual relationship with someone other than your husband or wife.

This ten-letter word, INFIDELITY, has caused many marriages to shipwreck. Some just fall to the bottom of the ocean, while some marriages wash ashore with hopes of being rescued, or making it off the deserted island.

Infidelity places most marriages right in the destructive path of divorce. It's sad, yet true. Most are damaged beyond repair. It is often asked, "Why would anyone want to sleep with someone else's spouse?" Well, many Christians simply allow the devil to distort their minds, while tricking a person to believe that it's okay this time.

Yes, lots of Christian men and women are guilty of ruining marriages and families. They seem to do it all for a little sex, or simply blame it on loneliness. Yep, I'm talking about saved, sanctified, Holy Ghost-filled saints. Regardless, if the adulterous affair is emotional or sexual, infidelity is wrong!

Infidelity is one of the main reasons Christian marriages disintegrate. They fall apart because the human flesh could not contain itself. Oftentimes, even as saints, we just fall right in the hands of the devil. Many people wonder why spouses cheat. It's not that they don't love their husbands or wives. Many of them just want to please their flesh. Most of the time, it's about having, or getting more, sex than they get at home. Extramarital affairs are often seen as a way to get away from the "normal" agenda of the marriage and family. And, if you ask the cheating spouse if they considered their mates good looking, most would say, "Yes." However, it's not about the beauty and sometimes it goes well beyond the sex.

Other issues and reasons are often attached to infidelity. Many think and say that men cheat more than women do simply because a man has more testosterone, which gives them stronger sex desires. Many reasons yet go unanswered as to why couples are unfaithful to their spouses. We will probably never know. These are just some possible reasons:

1. Is infidelity merely about sex?

2. Does infidelity start as an emotional link?

3. Is it the temptation of being at the wrong place at the wrong time?

4. Does a partner commit infidelity out of loneliness?

5. Is it that a husband or wife has gotten too busy dealing with the church or their careers?

6. Are spouses too busy taking care of the family and children, and not spending enough time together in the bedroom?

7. Does a husband no longer see his wife as the same sexy woman he married? Or, does he only view her as the "fat lady that wears the same robe and head rag" around the house?

8. Does a wife only see her husband as the old fat, bald, and boring man?

Regardless of how a spouse may see their mate, it's important to make time for great sex. Couples should never take their mates for granted. A spouse should make sure they meet their mate's sexual needs. As Mama used to say, "Whatever it took to get them, will be the same thing needed to keep them."

In other words, if you know your spouse had a healthy sexual appetite when you got married, then this ain't no time for dieting now! A healthy sexual relationship between husband and wife is a good thing. And, Christians, please be careful and remember that fasting and prayer is great, but don't always jump to partake when the church goes on a fast. Also, keep in mind that both the husband and wife must be in mutual agreement because we wouldn't want the old infidelity devil to creep on into the marriage. Remember, the bed should be undefiled as a married couple. According to Hebrews 13:4 (KJV), "Marriage is honorable in all and the bed undefiled; but whoremongers and adulterers God will judge."

Is infidelity forgivable? Yes, it is. Now, healing does take time, and some offended partners take longer than others do to forgive. I also know God is able to do anything. God made us, and He forgives us of our confessed sins, so why wouldn't a husband or wife forgive their spouse? I know that for some individuals, this sounds almost impossible to do, especially when a person has been let down by his or her spouse. But, as the scripture says in Mark 9:23, (NKJV), "Jesus said to him, 'If you can believe, all things are possible to him who believes.'"

I admire gospel singer and public figure, Tina Campbell (of the sister duo, Mary Mary). Tina chose to go public about her husband's infidelity issues. Wow! First, it takes a real woman and a real Christian woman to be bold enough to share her personal marital issues and pain with the entire world. Thank you, Tina. I salute you and your husband for your real commitment and desire to continue your marriage. May God forever bless your marriage, for you have encouraged many, as well as opening up the door of hope for troubled marriages.

As I said before, no marriage is without some type of issue. The world itself is not perfect. While we all strive for perfection, it just doesn't always turn out that way. Success of a marriage is up to the couple to work out any issues, as they arise. Any issue is critical when you feel like your marriage is failing.

Remember to ignore negative people who just want to be in your business. There will always be those captive audience critics who say, "If it was me, I would do this or that."

Well, they should all just zip their lips and keep their mouths off other folks' marriages. They should be praying, making sure their own grass stays green! Their marriage could be subject to failing, too. The devil doesn't care whose marriage he ruins. As in 1 Corinthians 10:12 (KJV), "Wherefore let him that thinketh he standeth, take heed lest he fall."

Notes

Chapter 6

Did You Hear from God?

Did you hear from God when you met the man or woman you married? Oftentimes, this is a question that, unfortunately, many couples forget to take into consideration before they leap into marriage. Many people, mainly women, tend to get so excited when they meet what they think is a good man.

Lots of single women immediately envisions spending the rest of their lives with a good man. But, oh, Ms. Thang, not so fast! Slow it up! Don't forget that now should be the time to fast and pray, more than ever.

Patience plays a vital part in hearing from God. However, listening and waiting on God will save you lots of headaches and heartaches.

You will find that marriage is almost the hardest job you will ever have. It runs a close second to raising children. However, you will also learn that no marriage is divorce proof. Everyone's marriage, at some given time, will face some type of challenge. So, why not be sure that you are equally yoked, and your spouse is willing to work hard at staying married.

Many individuals often fall in lust very quickly after meeting the person they think could be the perfect spouse. This leaves no real space or time to listen to God. If God were handing out extra ears, most people still wouldn't take the time to hear from Him, simply because we want what we want and how we want it. It's just human nature.

But, as the scripture says in Matthew 11:15 (KJV), "He that hath ears to hear, let him hear."

Many marriages could be spared from the evil deceptions of divorce. I'm sure that many divorcing spouses have regrets, simply because they did not wait to hear from God. Don't allow any man or woman to put a rush on you.

If he or she wants to get married in a hurry, they could be trying to cover something up. However, in most cases, time will certainly bring out the truth.

True colors come out, so keep your eyes and ears open; check out everything. Be your own detective...that is, while you're waiting to hear from God. Although you may compile your own questions, I have included a few you might want to include in your evaluations of Mr. or Ms. Right.

1. Is he/she a real woman or man of God?

2. Does he/she truly love God?

3. Does he/she study and read the word of God on a regular basis?

4. Does he/she attend church on a regular basis?

5. How many other women and men has he/she dated in their church?

6. Does he/she have a great relationship with their parents?

7. Has he/she ever been married?

8. Does he/she have any children? If so, what kind of relationship does he/she have with their children?

9. What is the kind of relationship he/she has with their baby's mama/baby's daddy?

10. Does he/she have a criminal background?

11. Does he/she have a source of income?

12. What is his/her credit score?

13. Are there any garnishments attached to wages?

14. Does he/she have goals, potential to move up in life?

15. Does he/she have personal insurance (health, death, car, etc.)?

16. Is he/she responsible and an independent adult?

17. Is he/she lazy?

Keep in mind these questions sound simple, but you would be surprised at how many people never ask such important questions to a possible spouse. Couples do not wait to hear from God, but they also don't even wait to get real answers from the person they want to marry.

Don't get in God's way and remember that He will give you what He wants when He wants you to have it. He knows everything. Maybe you are just not ready for marriage. He wants all of His children to be happy. According to Psalms 84:11 (KJV), "For the Lord God is a sun and shield: The Lord will give grace and glory: no good thing will he withhold from them that walk uprightly."

The Lord will always direct your path. However, we must allow Him to take the driver's seat.

It's very important that you know what you desire in a spouse.

Make a list of what you want and expect.

1. _____
   _____

2. _____
   _____

3. _____
   _____

4. _____
   _____

5. _____
   _____

6. _____
   _____

7. _____
   _____

8. _____
   _____

9. _____
   _____

10. _____
    _____

Now, make a list of what you will not settle for in a spouse:

1. _____
_____

2. _____
_____

3. _____
_____

4. _____
_____

5. _____
_____

6. _____
_____

7. _____
_____

8. _____
_____

9. _____
   _____

10. _____
    _____

Notes

_____
_____
_____
_____
_____
_____
_____
_____
_____
_____
_____
_____

Chapter 7

The Controversy of Marriage and Divorce

Both marriage and divorce are very controversial subjects these days, and society has adopted a new way of defining the institution called marriage. Why marriage works for some, and not so well for others? We will never really know. Marriage is a choice, and many couples do live up to the vows of for better or for worse. Divorce occurs every day, no matter who people choose to marry.

Today, more than ever, before we hear all sorts of debates about marriage, I would like to pose a few of the hot topic items. These are mostly issues I feel could help lower the statistics of divorces in the church. Perhaps, you would like to share them with your family, friends, church members, or whomever you feel may need them.

1. Should Christians be obligated to seek both pre- and post-marital counseling?

These days it seems to be quite simple and easy to say, "We're getting married," and then go to the courthouse and get a license.

Yep, it's that easy. Well, I guess you still need a viable signature from a judge or pastor. But that's usually how it goes. Most churchgoers fall right in line with the non- churchgoers. All you have to do is pay someone to perform a ceremony and bam! "Y'all be married."

What happened to the good old days where most churches/religions stated you must take mandatory classes for a certain amount of time? Classes should be for at least nine months prior to the marriage. Yes, I know it sounds harsh, but so are divorces.

And while it's a shame, some marriages don't even last nine days, nine weeks, nine months, nine rounds in the ring, or nine years.

It's just way too easy for a couple to change their minds about being committed and staying married. All a person has to do is go back to the courthouse, file a divorce document, and check the box that says irreconcilable differences. What the heck does irreconcilable differences really means anyway? The initiator goes on his or her merry way until the spouse is served their notice.

Yep, that seems way too easy for me. It should be mandatory for that same preacher/pastor or judge that signed the couple's marriage license to require the couple to do therapy prior to any divorce hearings or proceedings. The couple should not be granted anything until they have proven they have taken the necessary steps, hoping to save the marriage.

Why do I say this? Simply because so often we hear of couples who want to throw in the towel after only their first round in marriage. They haven't even been married long enough to know what a real marital issue is. Okay, yes, some divorces should be granted on the grounds and definition of automatic termination. And, only certain circumstances should qualify under such a definition. Yep, I know you are probably saying I'm a little crazy, but I'm not.

Divorces are out of control and changes to the bylaws for granting marriages and divorces are long overdue. Oh, yeah, and since it seems as though our new government leaders want to regulate everything, why don't they put some regulations on marriage and divorce?

Notes

2. ***Is it okay for Christians to have a current husband/wife in the same church where their former husband or wife worships?***

No. It is not good for former spouses and their remarried spouses to share the same home church. This could turn out to be a big old mess, right there in the church. I see this as being a messy baby mama/baby daddy drama that could possibly escalate to the tenth power.

Yes, I've seen similar drama with my own two eyes. Wife number one sitting on the back pew and wife number two sitting on the front row. Kids so confused they don't know if they are allowed to play with or talk to their other sisters and brothers. Even the children feel the tension. Don't be a messy Christian. After all, there are hundreds of churches all over the city, so simply find another one, please!

Notes

_____
_____
_____
_____

_____

_____

_____

_____

_____

_____

_____

_____

_____

3. *Should Christian leaders withdraw or take seats if they are having marital problems?*

Yes. Sit yourself down. As the famous quote says, "Charity starts at home and spreads abroad." How can you maintain a leadership position and be effective? How can parishioners follow someone who is having a problem leading? It just doesn't seem to work out too well.

Why? Great church leaders set the bar for the church. All eyes are on them. Parishioners look up to them. As a leader, it would be sad for everyone you are leading to fall because you did. Why be held accountable for a lost soul? If you are a mess, then you might lead your group into the mess and, as my pastor says, "That's just way too much mess."

Notes

4. Should Christians get prenups?

Yes, they should. We are human before we are Christian, and divorces do happen. If the couple acquired assets prior to the marriage, direct statements should reflect these facts. If the plan is to share assets upon dissolution of the marriage, state it in written documents. I bet if you take a survey, most people of my age and current generation would feel as I do.

It is also unfortunate that many couples tend to have major disagreements when it comes to finances. Communication is a great and necessary tool in any marriage, so why not communicate about prenuptials, just in case one day a spouse decides to throw in the towel? It's less to fight about, and perhaps this could allow both parties to remain friends. Having an understanding could help to minimize the feeling of deceit and trickery.

A prenup gives each individual a plan—the just in case theory. Although many might disagree with me, since prenups tend to automatically place a negative aura in the marriage. Regardless, if a person has much to lose, or gain, financially in a failing marriage, at least the couple will know the expectations since they agreed prior to the fighting. After all, it's what was agreed to previously.

So, when making a prenup, a couple should be honest and open about their true feelings. Okay, so you are probably thinking, *What about the bickering that normally comes with putting together a prenup?* Well, yes, it does happen. There are couples who decide not to get married at all. Okay! And, maybe not getting married is a good choice anyway. It saves a lot of heartache and pain that comes with any divorce. Just get over it and move on. You were saved. So what if you were subject to gain a house, a car, and a boat? Don't be so materialistic, with your sanctified self.

Notes

_____
_____
_____
_____
_____
_____

5. Should Christians be limited as to how many times they can get married?

Yes. Why? Some of y'all are out of control, with four living wives and twelve kids. Enough is enough. Get your act together. Face the facts. You've got issues, and you can't blame them all on someone else, either. You are a part of the reason, too. Stop blaming God and others for your shortcomings. Take time with your kids and, for God's sake, please help to support them financially. Be a real man and woman of God. No one should have to make you take care of your rightful responsibilities. In case you have forgotten, that means more than just picking the kids up and taking them for ice cream!

Regardless of whom you choose to marry, all parties should be ready. Ready to reciprocate. Ready to work hard. Marriage and raising children are actually two of the hardest jobs you could ever have. Be ready to sacrifice your time, your money, your selfish ways, and your me attitude.

Notes

Chapter 8

The Shame of Divorce in the Church

When Christians and Churchgoers divorce in the church, couples go through a period of feeling shame, embarrassment, and even mistrust of others. Quite often, they have feelings of no real support. I have seen and heard parishioners, church members, and even strangers, ready to get into the business of why Sister Bottle Top and Brother Bottle Top are getting a divorce.

Folks whispering, making all kinds of comments, wrong information mixed with bad and good information. It turns out to be a big mess. It doesn't take long before Sister or Brother Bottle Top stop going to their church. The pressures of the nosey folks, along with all the other stuff divorce brings, turns out to be way too much. Often, the divorcing man and/or woman will stop going to church all together, or will fellowship elsewhere, until the dust settles.

During my divorce process, I started to feel disconnected and uninvolved with my church. Perhaps, it was the shame of not having the perfect life or the perfect marriage. For those women who might be pregnant at the time of divorce, as it was in my case, it was quite hard to make it to church. It was a physical and a mental issue. I wondered if people had "heard the news."

I felt no one in my church would really understand. Now, my church, being a smaller family church, had no counseling center or support group that offered these types of services. Confidentiality is everything. When I think back, even if my church had an on-site counseling or family center, I probably would have never gone. I will admit that I was too embarrassed and hurt.

I didn't want to bother the pastor, for surely he already had enough on him, just being the pastor. I didn't even feel like I could talk to my First Lady. But, God is awesome. He knows exactly what we need and when we need it. He sent me to a church that was right down the street from my house. I hadn't even really taken notice of the church. I was okay with going, especially since it was the same denomination as my home church: C.O.G.I.C (Church of God in Christ).

It was all in God's plan. I thought I was going there to seek refuge and pray. I just needed a little strength to help me make it through to the next week. I remember having such a refreshing feeling, a feeling of "Wow."

Don't nobody know me here, I thought. No fear of shame or embarrassment. It was a fresh start. No one was in my personal business.

Notes

Chapter 9

Embrace Your Singleness

By now, it's probably all over the church you used to or still attend. Churchgoers have heard that you aren't wearing your ring anymore. That is, if you are still a member at the church where everything went down. And, it's okay to stay if that is what you feel. It's okay to admit that you are not married anymore.

Talking about it is healing in itself. Walk tall. Just remember that you aren't the first person in the church to get a divorce, and you sure won't be the last one, either. For whatever the reason it happened, it happened. And, until you are ready to go into detail about the divorce, it isn't anybody's business. Because we all know church folks are known for being nosey and messy. But, remember that talking about the devastation and getting it out starts the healing process and can help it to move a bit faster. As the scripture says, "And they overcame him by the blood of the Lamb and by the word of their testimony," Revelation 12:11(NKJV)

The first year after a divorce is often the hardest. It just takes time for you to transition back to being single again. Just the thought of being single again can be a bit scary and overwhelming. But, as the scripture says, "Cast thy burden upon the Lord, and He shall sustain thee," Psalms 55:22, and "Fear not, for I am with you; Be not dismayed, for I am your God. I will strengthen you, Yes, I will help you, I will uphold you with My righteous right hand," Isaiah 41:10 (NKJV). God will strengthen you. Yes, He will help you. He will uphold you with his right hand. So, take it slow. Because God is surely in control.

Despite your pain and disappointment, God has even a bigger blessing for you.

Don't sit around the house, moping. Stop wasting so much energy on focusing on the negative. Pick yourself up and dust yourself off. Get up and get out of the house. It's more to life than going to church and work. Perhaps take this time to join a support group, join a club, or do volunteer work. Visit the sick and shut-in. Sometimes, when we see others who have issues greater than ours, it makes us count our blessings.

Here are just a few tips/activities to do:

1. Look into a mirror every day, several times a day, and say, "I am a survivor. I will make it through this. God, I love you, and I love myself."

2. Take that long-awaited trip (one that you have always talked about).

3. Go on a retreat.

4. Hang out with friends.

5. Do a spa day, massage, facial, etc.

6. Buy a new outfit.

7. Get a new hairdo.

8. Change your lipstick color.

9. Treat yourself to a five-star restaurant.

10. Take a class (cooking, art, dancing, sewing)

11. Go back to school (earn another degree).

But, most of all, please use your time wisely. Keep in mind that growth and pain seem to go together. Look at it this way, when a woman gives birth to a baby, there is so much labor and pain in the beginning. But, oh the joy, beauty, and life that comes out of all that pain. God gives life and He gives it more abundantly.

In order for us to step into our own destiny and purpose in life, we must endure a certain amount of pain. Pain has really proven itself a part of life's growth process. Keep in mind that what might look like a setback in life is really a setup, a mandatory push to your next level.

Remember: God truly loves you, and He knows you. He won't place more on you than you can bear. "And we know that in all things God works for the good of those who love him, who have been called according to his purpose," Romans 8:28 (NIV). According to Jeremiah 29:11 (NIV), "'For I know the plans I have for you,' declares the Lord, 'plans to prosper you and not to harm you, plans to give you hope and a future.'"

If you take the first step, God will take the next. Allow Him to speak to you. Listen to what He tells you.

God's got your back, and I know there is nothing too hard for Him. Happiness belongs to you. Despite how you might be feeling right now, remember to keep God first in your life. Get a prayer partner or make time to spend alone with God. For this, too, shall pass. Keep your head up and keep a smile on your face. Stop regretting. Forgive yourself and let the healing begin.

Always try to think positive thoughts while continuing to pray for peace of mind. It will make you feel better. As the word says, "Thou wilt keep him in perfect peace, whose mind is stayed on thee: because he trusteth in thee," Isaiah 26:3 (KJV).

My sisters and brothers, continue to trust in God. "For the peace of God, which transcends all understanding, will guard your hearts and your minds in Christ Jesus," Philippians 4:7 (NIV).

Hold on.

"For the race is not given to the swift and neither to the strong but to him that endureth till the end," Ecclesiastes 9:11.

I am a witness that God can, and will, pull you through what seems to be the hardest test of your life. I encourage women and men all over the world to embrace your time of singleness. "Do you!" Most of all, I encourage you to love and support family and friends, who might be attempting to get through the trial of a divorce. Don't put down one another. Put your arms out, extending a helping hand to do whatever it is that you can do. No person is exempt from falling and becoming a victim of the divorce epidemic.

At this time in your life, setting goals is important. Take time and rekindle any abandoned aspirations.

List five personal goals and dates of when you plan to accomplish them.

1. _____
   _____

2. _____
   _____

3. _____

4. _____

5. _____

Remind yourself that you are more than a conqueror. Now, list five strong words that would describe you.

1. _____
2. _____
3. _____
4. _____
5. _____

List any steps you feel will be necessary to take your life to the next level.

_____
_____
_____
_____
_____

Notes

Chapter 10

Pieces of Me

I grew up in the inner city of Los Angeles in a nice, middle-class family and home. My parents were married more than fifty years. I was the youngest of three older sisters. Considered church kids, we went to church with my mother, at least a few times a week. This was my way of life.

Mom always hung out with the saints, and my dad liked to go to the racetrack. My parents worked outside the home, and neither let anything get in the way of doing what they enjoyed. This usually meant they often went their separate ways. Despite their differences, though, they remained together and raised four strong women. They even adopted my little sister, well into their senior years. They were great parents. I admired their commitment to marriage. "'Til death did they part."

In 1994, life was going great. At age twenty-four, I purchased my own home. I was working as a second-grade schoolteacher and working for a major airline. All I needed was a tall, handsome man. So, in 1996, I met one of my students' dad. He volunteered on a field trip. I had no idea this second-grade student's father had been checking me out. He started going to church with me, and, several months later, he surprised me during prayer service by asking me to marry him in front of the entire church congregation.

Several months later, we got married, and I moved into the big house. Life just couldn't get any better. My husband was tall, dark, handsome, smart, and financially stable—gosh, it was the perfect picture. We were two young entrepreneurs doing our thang. A woman could have only dreamed about a life like this. We took vacations, planned to have kids, and the whole nine yards.

From the outside looking in, we had it going on. Then, all of a sudden, the earthquake shook and epidemic struck. It hit hard. Out of nowhere, I found my life turning upside down. I could not believe what was happening. My wonderful life was over, even before it had begun. And, being with child made the whole situation worse.

After my divorce, I became something I never wanted to be—alone and a single parent. I was sad and depressed. I felt as though someone had just ripped my heart out and left me for dead. My heart was bleeding, and no one could do anything to save me from my pain. I questioned God repeatedly, as to why He allowed something like this to happen to me.

I was ashamed, embarrassed, and hid my divorce from many people. Even people right in my church. Being at the lowest point of my life, I wanted to avoid people who knew I had not been married for too long.

I prayed and I cried, hoping God would fix everything. I wanted my marriage back. I played Donnie McClurkin's "Stand" so much until I broke it. I told God I was standing on

His word. Despite being torn, I went to work every day with a smile on my face. Many thought and said I had it going on.

Nonetheless, if they only knew that I was in a deep depression. There were days when I thought about ending my life, as well as my child's life. I felt God had let me down. I felt the church had let me down, too. I had no one to talk to other than my mom, sisters and girlfriends. I wondered why we didn't have a counseling center at my church. Maybe my marriage could have been saved. In this case, I would say, I married a man without first taking time to consult with God. I wasn't even thinking about checking with God. I just figured on the way to almost thirty, I had already checked things off on my list, and marriage was next.

I was way too excited about having the big beautiful ring and wedding ceremony. And, beautiful it was. But, I also learned that If God doesn't put it together, then it would fail. As a couple, we were unequally yoked, spiritually. We were good on the other stuff, but I had missed one of the most important items I had not included on my list.

Later, after joining my new church, I began to view life in a different aspect. I started feeling a bit better and singing in the choir. I met a new man, however, he actually saw me while visiting my church. The last thing on my mind was a man. But, he found me one Sunday at the afternoon church service. Many weeks went by before he was finally successful in obtaining my phone number. We talked and courted many times before I finally opened up to him. Funny, we became the best of friends. Everyone in my circle knew and loved him. He was a real church going man. Saved and sanctified. I mean, his entire family was churchgoers just like mine. We both grew up under the same faith and denomination. I was so grateful to have a person like him. He helped me take my mind off the divorce drama. We could talk and pray about anything.

At age forty, I knew I wanted to have another baby. So, I became pregnant while in graduate school, and we had a baby. We dated thirteen years before attempting to say, "I do," but we never finalized it.

In both relationships, I now realize I did not check with God. I did not wait to hear from Him. I just did what I wanted to do. I knew my plans, and I was sticking to them.

I got in the driver's seat of my life, but can't nobody beat God's driving. If I could have a redo on a few things, I'll admit,

I would certainly change some of them. However, out of all my life's experiences, I have grown mentally and spiritually. I now understand many things. Proverbs 4:7 (NIV), "The beginning of wisdom is this: Get wisdom. Though it cost all you have, get understanding."

I have no regrets because, despite my taking over God's steering wheel of my life, He is giving me a second chance, another chance at my purpose and my destiny. As I reflect, I know these trials and life experiences have helped to make me into who I am today. I take nothing in life for granted, for He has surely been good to me. I thank and praise Him for using me as His vessel. Without Him, I could do nothing and I would fail. He has allowed me to move forward on my dream of helping others.

Notes

C

Chapter 11

Why I Will Never Marry Again

At age forty-nine, I am taking a stance in choosing never to marry again. Now wait one minute and hear me out before you start judging me. I realize many traditional church-going Christians will ridicule me for saying that marriage just isn't for me. But, I look at it this way. Everyone has a choice, and my choice is never to marry again.

We must learn to respect a person's choice. For every man and woman must live life for self.

I'm happy as a single parent. I'm a great mother of two kids, ages nineteen and nine. Life is great. I have time to focus on my children. Their wants and needs are important to me, as well as quality time together.

I have chosen to commit to God first, followed by my family and my business. I have chosen to take the opportunity and time to work on me. My dreams! My desires! My wishes! So, call me a little selfish, it's okay. It's my choice, and I choose to commit to myself. Commitment to one's self is important and commitment to others is just as serious. Where there is no true commitment, there is no great relationship.

That one problem plagues marriages today, causing them to fail. I always hear people saying that they want to be married, but I'm not sure they really do. Some just really want to focus on themselves and not change their ways or habits for anyone along the way. Lots of times, we are not honest with ourselves, which means we set ourselves up for destruction and disaster.

I don't feel the need to be married to justify living a satisfying life. For me, the eight-letter word (MARRIAGE) is not the missing link in my life. Marriage is not necessary to help make me feel whole or complete. I have learned to live for myself, and by myself. My life is happy. It's pleasant, and God is good.

Marriage. I've been there and done that, you could say one-and-one-half times. Don't worry about the half! I'm good and I don't see anything wrong with having a friend, seeing how wonderful he is. But, at this point in my life, I don't feel the need to be married. At this time, I'm choosing to help others, and I am committed to doing so. When you bless others, God blesses you. I want all the blessings that God has for me. With all the commitments already on my plate, I really don't have much time for anything else. Something would have to give, and I am not sacrificing any of my commitments just to say that I'm married. I will not get caught up with that again.

So, I urge those of you that might feel as I do, stick to your heart. Don't worry about what others may say, or think if you choose never to marry again. People will always have something to say. After all, I bet the ones talking are the main ones with problems at home. They should all just mind their married businesses. As Bobby Brown say, "It's my prerogative!" Just as long as I'm happy.

Happiness is important to all mankind. In fact, it can actually promote long life. Humans and animals can actually die from a lonely or broken heart. So, again, I believe if a person is truly happy without marriage, fine. Marriage does not define happiness on an individual level, and lots of people have found happiness without it.

Notes

Chapter 12

Healing and Feeling Better

My mind, my heart, and my soul have been healed, delivered, and set free. At one time in my life, everything inside of me hurt. It was an indescribable hurt. Now, I will admit, because there had to be a (kinship) relationship, the devil tried to torment me. But, I rebuked him and spoke the word.

God said that He would never put more on you than you can bear. Although this tragic event happened over eighteen years ago, I have forgiven others and myself. We forgive, but sometimes it's hard to forget. I praise and thank God for His Revelation, for I now truly understand why He took me through it, but brought me out of all of this.

Understand that you had to endure that pain in order for you to receive restoration and a re-evaluation of life itself. It may be hard to understand how something so good could be so bad. For all of your questions and tears, God has chosen to use me as a vessel for you. Back then, I didn't even think I would make it. But, my soul looks back and wonders just how I got over it.

The devil doesn't like me, and I don't like him either. I passed this test. For without the test, there would be no testimony. I made it out. I'm supposed to be dead. I hope you understand why I must be about my God's business. I'm on an assignment. If you can only keep the faith and hang on in there, God can, and will, bring you out.

Don't let the devil take you down. He wants to destroy you. Get up! And fight! Fight for your life! Don't stop swinging until you win! Pray, scream, yell, and cry. It's all right. It's all a part of the fight. The Lord, our God, loves you and no one else compares.

Today, I am a much stronger woman than when I was thirty years old. I take nothing in life for granted. My whole approach is different. I am happy to say I still have love for the Black man. However, I have learned that regardless of color, men are men, and that's who they will be. I had to learn how to love again. I also had to learn how to find my inner strength. When no one else was around, I learned how to sit, wait, and listen. Peace comes from within.

When you finally face that fact, you, too, will be on your way to healing and feeling better. You must face the fact that you are divorced, and be determined not to allow anything, or anyone, to disturb your inner peace. When you find a deep sense of peace, it will start shining from the inside out. Others will begin noticing there is something different about you. Others will want to know why you are always so happy. Let them know, as the old song goes, "This joy that I have, the world didn't give it to me."

God is the giver of joy and peace, and He will give you peace beyond your own understanding. When little issues flare up, it's nothing but Satan wanting to steal your joy. Just tell him to get behind you. Give it to God, and He will handle it. Just keep on telling yourself that this, too, shall pass.

Notes

Conclusion

Marriage is not meant for everyone. Having or raising children is not for everyone. Society, along with its progressive outlook and notion of what is a perfect life, continues to sway individuals to think something is wrong if life aspirations don't include living up to how they define it. For decades, a perfect standard life has been "the nuclear family," one which includes husband, wife, two kids, and the family pet. When you add power, prestige and money, one is persuaded to believe he or she must ascertain the

"American Dream." Unfortunately, the pressure of having to live up to such expectations tends to leave individuals feeling hopeless and inadequate. However, achieving the Dream does not always equate to a happy and fulfilled life. Being married does not necessarily equal wholeness. One is a whole number all by itself. God created everyone whole and unique in His own image. So, it's okay to choose to live your best life, even when it looks different when compared to most. Remember, you can live a saved, satisfied, single, married or divorced life and still be whole and content with life.

ABOUT THE AUTHOR

Mable Alyse Manning is a family therapist/mentor/life coach, motivational speaker, and the C.E.O. of Significant Women Making Changes Women's Group. As a former educator, she has always desired to help others become the best they can be and to rise above life's difficult challenges.

Mable Alyse is an acclaimed anointed singer and songwriter. She grew up singing in the Church of God In Christ. She has performed with several national gospel musical/theatre productions, as well as with various artists, such as Cece Winans, Beau Williams, The O'Jays, Dr. Dre, Snoop, Ice Cube, and the Notorious B.I.G.

Mable Alyse is a 30-year employee in the Airline industry, a divorcee, and mother of two dynamic, wonderful children: Ryan (daughter, 19 years old) who has completed her first year at BIOLA University and Andrew (son, nine years old) who has proven to be a young, gifted basketball player. She loves spending time with her children and says, "They are both my "gifts" from God."

Because of Mable Alyse's firsthand experience of what it's like to go through a divorce and being in the church, she wrote Divorce in the Church with the hopes of helping to heal lives across America. She believes people are hurting and often need someone other than friends or family to reach out to; therefore, she knows that restoration comes from the help of outside interventions. Her God-given destiny and purpose in life is to continue to inspire individuals to "live their life, never give up when things get tough, and know that they're going to make it."

www.ingramcontent.com/pod-product-compliance
Lightning Source LLC
Chambersburg PA
CBHW031426290426
44110CB00011B/542